SUMM

How to Win Friends

and Influence People

by Dale Carnegie

Summary by: Napoleon Hook

ISBN: 9781717987211.

Table of Contents

Introduction	**5**
PART I: Fundamental Techniques in Handling People	**6**
Principle 1: Don't criticize, condemn, or complain.	6
Principle 2: Give honest and sincere appreciation.	8
Principle 3: Arouse in the other person an eager want.	9
PART II: Six Ways to Make People Like You	**10**
Principle 1: Become genuinely interested in other people.	10
Principle 2: Smile.	12
Principle 3: Remember that a person's name is to that person the sweetest and most important sound in any language.	13
Principle 4: Be a good listener. Encourage others to talk about themselves.	15
Principle 5: Talk in terms of the other person's interests.	17
Principle 6: Make the other person feel important — and do it sincerely.	18
PART III: Win People to Your Way of Thinking	**19**
Principle 1: The only way to get the best of an argument is to avoid it.	19
Principle 2: Show respect for the other person's opinions. Never say, "You're wrong."	21
Principle 3: If you are wrong, admit it quickly and emphatically.	23
Principle 4: Begin in a friendly way.	24
Principle 5: Get the other person saying "yes, yes" immediately.	25
Principle 6: Let the other person do a great deal of the talking.	26
Principle 7: Let the other person feel that the idea is his or hers.	27

Principle 8: Try honestly to see things from the other person's point of view.   28

Principle 9: Be sympathetic with the other person's ideas and desires.   29

Principle 10: Appeal to the nobler motives.   30

Principle 11: Dramatize your ideas.   31

Principle 12: Throw down a challenge.   32

PART IV: Be a Leader: How to Change People Without Giving Offense or Arousing Resentment   33

Principle 1: Begin with praise and honest appreciation.   33

Principle 2: Call attention to people's mistakes indirectly.   34

Principle 3: Talk about your own mistakes before criticizing the other person.   35

Principle 4: Ask questions instead of giving direct orders.   36

Principle 5: Let the other person save face.   37

Principle 6: Praise the slightest improvement and praise every improvement. Be "hearty in your approbation and lavish in your praise."   38

Principle 7: Give the other person a fine reputation to live up to.   39

Principle 8: Use encouragement. Make the fault seem easy to correct.   40

Principle 9: Make the other person happy about doing the thing you suggest.   41

Conclusion   42

Check Out Other Summaries   43

Introduction

The book, *How to Win Friends and Influence People* which was issued in 1936, is probably the ideal self-aid book for everyone. Dale Carnegie authored the book which provides many extremely important propositions based on social communications and greatly successful methods of handling people. All the theories are arranged into four groups: Basic methods of managing people, techniques of forming people as you are, ways of impressing people by your opinions, and the effective ways to be a controller: The effective ways of changing others without making them uncomfortable.

The book has achieved the reputation of being a global bestseller as more than 15 million copies of this book have been sold after it came into the market. This can be evidence of the fact that the methods described in the book are applicable for all time. The book can be the ultimate guide to help you learn about communication skills and the ways of enhancing the quality of relationships with others.

All the main methods and essential terms of Carnegie's book have been gathered into this short version which will work as a summary for you. This abstract will surely help you even if you don't read the full version but we recommend that you read through Carnegie's book for detailed understanding.

PART I: Fundamental Techniques in Handling People

Principle 1: Don't criticize, condemn, or complain.

Even if people do something incorrectly, they don't condemn themselves. So your job is not to condemn them as well.

It is natural for a person to be defensive when they are being criticized as it surely will hurt their pride. You should consider criticism as a risk as it will only make short-term changes.

You need to regard other people as emotional instead of logical when you are working with them.

Therefore, you should avoid criticism. Otherwise, the problems will only increase. If you hurt others' ego, they will try to harm you in order to defend themselves.

It is easy to get caught up in criticism but it takes a lot of effort to avoid and excuse yourself from getting involved in it. You need to think logically about the reasons behind their actions instead of blaming them. This will result in empathy and forbearance.

Ways of applying this method:

If you think that other people's actions are affecting you, restrain yourself from criticizing.

You need to consider their reasoning for doing whatever it is that is not acceptable to you. After you think about those things you need to convince yourself that even if it's their fault, you should consider forgiving them and be kind. This process will make everything easier and better for you.

Principle 2: Give honest and sincere appreciation.

What determines the difference between a human being and an animal is the strong desire for feeling needed by other humans. But still, we fail to show admiration to others.

Many people fall into a deep depression when they think they are not needed. Imagine what great things can be earned by showing honest and genuine admiration.

You need to understand the difference between insincere praise and honest praise. Flattery comes from the mouth when honest praising comes from the heart. You need to be honest, sincere, and kind with your words as flattery will only make things worse. You need to analyze the qualities the person has before making him work for you and gaining profit. Praise them for their good traits and make them understand that you noticed their fine qualities. Only then will they respect your praises and work.

Ways of applying this method:

Think about some honest feedback about the person you want respect from before you talk to them.

If it's hard for you to come up with some positive appreciations right away, develop the habit of analyzing people's qualities while communicating with them. It will make it much easier later.

Principle 3: Arouse in the other person an eager want.

The first step of getting work done by others is making them want to do it. In other words, make them eager to do the work on their own. There are many ways to do this, but you need to choose the best methods. If you treat others to do it, the consequences will not be in your favor. If you can arouse their eagerness of doing these good works by being kind to them, your reputation will be enriched.

This process is for the benefit of both parties. You should not consider this as a way of manipulating others; the results will be devastating. You need to consider the other party's gains and should not be selfish.

Ways of applying this method:

Before you try to convince someone to work for you, stop yourself and analyze the reasons for him to do the work—things the individual can achieve from the deal and the ways of adapting the work for their benefit.

In the case of emailing someone, asking them to do you a favor, you need to use words that will make it look like it's in their best interest to help.

PART II: Six Ways to Make People Like You

Principle 1: Become genuinely interested in other people.

It takes less effort to be curious about other people than making other people curious about you. And, it is a great way to meet new friends.

There are so many people out there who want to impress everyone around them; this takes a lot of effort and time. The goal is to get people to like them and become their friends because of the things they have or the cool personality they try to show. In reality, it just does not work that way. People in general are more interested in themselves and they do not have time to show real interest in others. This process will only bring fake friends in your life. It will only attract people who want something from you. As soon as you can't offer it to them, they disappear.

The very first step to making true friends is to greet them sincerely and warmly with an excited voice that expresses to them how much you like them. Even if it's a phone call, use a tone that shows your interest in that person. Do things that show your attention and effort toward speaking with them; show that you really care.

The most important thing to consider here is that you are sincere with your feelings. Both people need to be interested.

Ways of applying this method:

When you are communicating with the person you want to be friends with, you need to try to know that person better. Ask questions, and try to learn about the things you do not already know about that person. Show your sincerity.

Try to have conversations where not only you are interested but the other person is also interested. If the other person talks about his or her hobbies and interests, encourage that person to talk. You might just find out about some things you have in common!

Principle 2: Smile.

The next step to making a good impression on someone is to smile warmly while starting a conversation with them. The way you act speaks about what kind of person you are and the smile you give shows that you are truly happy to see them.

If you want to be friends with someone, give them the smile which says that you happy to see them and are interested in them as well. Bring your actions and words together. If you don't smile warmly, it might look like you are not happy to see them. You need to be sincere in your feelings as it will give a natural and sincere smile as well.

Giving a genuine smile may cost close to nothing but it will surely bring you much more than you can even imagine. It will work as an invitation to others that says "hey I want to be your friend!" There are many people who do not get to see a warm smile every day. When you will smile at them warmly, they will consider you as a friendly person and want to talk to you more. They will realize that you bring them happiness.

Ways of applying this method:

All you need to do is smile whenever you see someone regularly who looks interesting as a potential new friend—and try to be relaxed while smiling.

Principle 3: Remember that a person's name is to that person the sweetest and most important sound in any language.

The name gives every individual an identity which separates them in this crowded world. People tend to be proud of their name. We meet so many people on different occasions and it's hard to remember all the names. This often leads us to forget the names of people afterward.

Remembering people by their name and mentioning their name while talking to them is a way of showing respect and if you don't remember their name or pronounce it incorrectly, it shows disrespect.

The most important thing for you to do is to remember their name. If you remember the name of a person, it will show them that they are important to you. Remembering people's names is a big deal in every environment. It does not matter if it's your personal life or business life, if you put in the effort to remember others' names, they will put in the effort to remember yours as well. This process works like magic to every person as you are differentiating that individual from others.

Ways of applying this method:

You need to try sincerely to memorize the name of the individual. You can say the name several times in your mind the moment you meet that person and also relate the name with some qualities that person has.

If the name is difficult and unique, all you need to do is tell him or her to spell and pronounce the name again for you. After a short time you will be able to remember it easily and it will seem natural.

Principle 4: Be a good listener. Encourage others to talk about themselves.

Another quality you will need for being friends with someone includes being a nice conversation partner and listener. People want others to listen to them and give value to their words. You need to let them speak and allow them to feel at ease with you. This way they will come to think that you are someone they can talk to whenever they need someone to listen.

It is important to listen to what the other person is saying not only in your business but also in your personal life. If you can do this, people will listen when you talk and value your opinions.

If your purpose is to become a conversation partner with someone with whom you want to form a long-term relationship, the quality of listening patiently is a must. You need to listen and also concentrate on the meaning as well.

On the other hand, if you tend to interrupt while others are talking to you, they will surely avoid having conversations with you.

Avoid talking only about yourself while you are talking to other people. This will cause them to think of you as a selfish person.

Ways of applying this method:

Try to compare the amount of time you spend talking with the amount of time spent by the other while you are talking to them. It will help you to notice your traits of talking and listening to others. You need to talk less and listen more.

You need to identify the reasons behind your excessive talking. After you know the reasons, correct them according to your understanding and encourage the other person to talk more. Ask them more about themselves.

Principle 5: Talk in terms of the other person's interests.

Everyone will be willing to talk to you if your interests are similar to theirs. You can easily converse with others if you know what they are interested in.

If you want to hold someone's attention and try to talk to them, you need to analyze that person. Try to identify useful information while talking to them. You need to know what that person is interested in and find out if there are any similarities between your interests to extend the conversation.

Ways of applying this method:

It is easy to find information, thanks to social media. You need to do a little bit of research on this person's interests. If you know about the preferences of the individual, you will know what subjects will make him want to talk and what you should talk about.

This process will develop a good atmosphere for the two of you to carry on a conversation that both of you can relate to.

Principle 6: Make the other person feel important – and do it sincerely.

People bend to present themselves as an important individual to others. It's human nature. People want to be accepted by others. When someone gives them this feeling of importance, they realize that the person is accepting him.

Giving importance to someone also means acknowledging that person's ability and existence. Human being aims to clarify their existence in this world. Consequently, you need to give out what you expect to receive back from others. Try giving people sincere feelings of importance, value, and sympathy and only then you will get the same in return.

If you tend to do otherwise, it will only bring you misery.

Ways of applying this method:

Look around you and search for someone who needs some kind words from a warm heart. Try to make someone who is having troubles happy.

Try to practice this every day and you can easily make people around you feel important and needed.

PART III: Win People to Your Way of Thinking

Principle 1: The only way to get the best of an argument is to avoid it.

Avoiding an argument is the best solution to an argument. When you argue with a person, what you are trying to do is to prove that person wrong. And that person will try to prove you wrong to save their own pride. But if you think that proving him wrong would be the best thing to do, that is a mistake. If you prove yourself right, you will be hurting your opponent's pride. They will feel inferior and will be unwilling to work with you.

There is a saying which states that only showing love and affection can erase hatred. So, whenever you get involved in arguments, try to follow these instructions:

- Accept the opinions of others. You may learn something from it as well.
- Don't let your anger or emotions control you and your judgment.
- Don't interrupt your opponent and pay attention to what they have to say.
- Try to find those things that you agree with them about.
- Try to make your opponent relax by saying they are your faults as well.
- Consider their opinions.
- Take as much time as needed. Do not rush things.

Ways of applying this method:

Avoid complicating things more by criticizing the opinions of others. Think carefully about what your opponent stated and take the time to analyze their words properly.

Principle 2: Show respect for the other person's opinions. Never say, "You're wrong."

Sometimes words can hurt more than actions. When someone does something wrong, directly telling them with words will hurt a person's pride more than showing them with a friendly gesture. The other person will never agree with the statement right away and it will lead to an argument. If someone happens to be wrong, do not correct him right away by telling them how wrong they are. It will hurt that individual's intelligence and ego. Take as much time as you need and do it as delicately as possible.

You need to choose your words very carefully. Use kind words, so that the other person cannot deny your proposal of correcting the mistake.

You need to work skillfully as there are not many people who like to be put on the spot, no matter how logical the explanations sound. Avoid an argument even if it is not aggressive.

Ways of applying this method:

If someone is wrong and it's making you uneasy, the first thing for you to do is not to get angry or hasty. Do not accuse them of making a mistake. Ask them questions and let them explain their logic. Make them understand plausibly where they have gone wrong.

Ask for permission to explain your perception of the situation before stating your opinion so that the opponent does not mind listening to your point of view.

Principle 3: If you are wrong, admit it quickly and emphatically.

Admitting your own mistakes always brings satisfaction. If you think you have said something wrong or made a mistake, always apologize and correct the wrongs before others correct it. This behavior will enhance your good sides and the polite behavior will make people like you more as well.

Your opinions will help you to gain trust and if there are any mistakes, correcting them after apologizing will certainly make you appear reliable. Therefore, you need to admit your own mistakes, which is much easier than arguing to make it look right.

<u>Ways of applying this method:</u>

Always try your best to identify your own mistakes and apologize for them first.

Think about solutions and convey them to everyone. It will make you more reliable and responsible.

Principle 4: Begin in a friendly way.

It is not up to you whether someone will like you or not. But you can make an effort to influence their opinion. A friendly approach is always welcomed by other people. If you approach others in a warm and friendly way, it is more likely that they will also welcome you.

People will take a chance to get to know you if you approach them in a friendly way. Kindness is always sought after by human beings.

<u>Ways of applying this method:</u>

Speak calmly and try to develop an affectionate conversation. Do not talk about things like work right away. You need to make the person feel calm and relaxed on a personal level and then talk about work later after you get to know more about each other.

Principle 5: Get the other person saying "yes, yes" immediately.

If you need to make a deal with others, the first thing you need to do is to find if your opinion and your opponent's opinion have any similarities. Do not try to highlight the points that you both disagree on. It will just make it worse and lead to aggressive conversation.

Make your opponents realize that your and their motives are not different and that there is some middle ground. Try to get a positive response from the very beginning which will set a positive environment.

This process needs several positive responses and the more "yes" you can get the better.

This process will help to avoid hurting your opponent's pride and they will feel positive about your opinion.

Ways of applying this method:

Whenever you get into an argument, try asking the questions where the opponent needs to answer with 'yes' and get at least two 'yes' answers before stating your opinion. This will show them that there is a middle ground between both of your opinions.

Principle 6: Let the other person do a great deal of the talking.

You need to speak as little as possible. Encourage the opponent to do the talking most of the time. Listen to and concentrate on his or her points and do not stop even if what they are saying is wrong. This way they will develop a new found respect towards you and they will also give more attention to what you say.

The less you say, the more value gets added to your words. Humans feel the urge to share their thoughts and they want some personal attention. They want people to listen to what they have to say. If someone pays attention to his or her opinion, he or she will also pay attention to them.

You need to listen to whatever they say and concentrate on their words.

Ways of applying this method:

Try to restrain yourself from talking unnecessarily. Hold your desire to talk too much and try to be at ease while listening to others.

Wait patiently and let them talk to you.

Principle 7: Let the other person feel that the idea is his or hers.

Try to convince the other party that all his or her actions are decided by themselves and you do not have any influence on them. If people think they are being influenced or other people are controlling them, they tend to get angry and do not listen anymore.

Instead of telling them what to do or how to do it, guide their way and make them realize that everything was done by them on their own accord.

Ways of applying this method:

You need to lead people in the way you want them to go technically. In other words, do not literally ask them the main topic of the conversation but ask the right questions which will lead them to the main issue.

Principle 8: Try honestly to see things from the other person's point of view.

You do not need to be wise to make fun of other people's opinions. But you need to be wise enough not to criticize even if the person is completely wrong.

Try to think what the other person could be thinking when he or she stated the wrong opinion. Do not point it out immediately. It will hurt their ego. Treat them the same way you want to be treated if you were wrong.

Try to think from a different angle and then inspire them to correct it. Direct them to make their mistakes correct and in this way, they will come to respect you.

Ways of applying this method:

When you talk to others, try to analyze the way they think. If you need their help, think before you ask them. Come up with possible answers you can get and think about the reasons behind it, and what the other person might gain from it.

Principle 9: Be sympathetic with the other person's ideas and desires.

When someone is being irrational with you, you need to calm yourself before you make any comment. Think about the environment and try to realize that the person is not at fault, but it is the environment that influenced him to be the way he is or the cause of mistakes. You should feel sympathy for that person. Every person on earth wants sympathy.

If you give them affection and sympathy, they will also return the favor.

Ways of applying this method:

When you are involved in an argument and do not agree with others, think about them first. Think about how frustrating and monotonous their lives might be. Try to show them affection and give them a warm welcome.

Principle 10: Appeal to the nobler motives.

When you need to influence other people's opinions, you need to give them greater reasons. Otherwise, they will not be influenced.

The first thing you need to do is listen to their statements. What they want to say is important to them. So you need to listen to them and make them know that you are interested in what is important to them. Then try to show them the positive sides where you agree with them as well.

Ways of applying this method:

While talking to others, concentrate on what they are trying to imply and analyze them carefully. Think about the positive and good things. Afterword's tell them about those good sides and agree on it.

Principle 11: Dramatize your ideas.

Drama always captures attention. If you want someone's attention, make your words and actions dramatic. This will make your expressions long lasting as well. People will pay more attention to it if it's dramatic. Otherwise, they will think it's another common concept and ignore it. The drama will add value to your opinion.

You need to spice up your words with emotion and logic. Make it realistic and captivating while presenting. This process will capture great attention and make people listen to it.

Ways of applying this method:

You need to be as creative as possible in order to make the presentation or your statement more appealing to the audience. Enhance the emotion while presenting the idea.

Principle 12: Throw down a challenge.

Challenges always bring excitement and develop the urge of winning within people. This motivates every human and eases the bonds between one another.

You need to make the works challenging at a level which will make people motivated to do the work. This way the subordinates will be working happily without getting bored.

Ways of applying this method:

Think of ways which will stimulate the urge of winning within a group of people. This motivation will help to get work done without any problem.

PART IV: Be a Leader: How to Change People Without Giving Offense or Arousing Resentment

Principle 1: Begin with praise and honest appreciation.

If there is no other option but to comment on the mistakes of an individual, you need to start with something positive and something which is in his or her favor. It will be easier for him or her to take the negative comments after the positive ones.

Ways of applying this method:

You need to consider the feelings of other people before giving them negative feedback. You need to use a soft tone and start with positive feedback so that they feel at ease and take the negative ones calmly.

Principle 2: Call attention to people's mistakes indirectly.

All people are different and they tend to deal with mistakes differently. When you point out their mistakes, you need to be indirect. Otherwise, it can hurt their ego. You need to understand the person before commenting on his or her mistakes to check how he or she deals with it.

Ways of applying this method:

Use kind words as much as possible and encourage him to do better work. The wording needs to be carefully chosen.

Principle 3: Talk about your own mistakes before criticizing the other person.

If you talk about how you used to make mistakes, it will help others to realize that you are not only criticizing that person but also sincerely want him to do well. It will also reduce the depression level for that individual and he or she will be motivated to do well in the future.

Ways of applying this method:

Before giving bad feedback, think about how you would feel if you were in that person's place. Think about all the mistakes you have made and work according to the answers you get. It will help you to be a good monitor.

Principle 4: Ask questions instead of giving direct orders.

Taking orders from others can be very frustrating for all. If you can convert your orders to make them sound more like a request or ask questions instead this will help people to get motivated.

You need to be very technical with your choice of words. You wording needs to be kind and affectionate as well. The way you give instructions to people, the result will depend on the way in which you give out the instructions. Consequently, you need to motivate them with your words.

If you ask encouraging questions it will help to make their creative minds work.

Ways of applying this method:

Stop yourself while you are about to use force when asking others to do work for you. You need to be careful with your words. Try to give instruction by asking questions. Refrain from using force.

Principle 5: Let the other person save face.

When you realize your statement is absolutely correct and what the other person is saying is incorrect, you need to hold your excitement of hurting their pride. You need to be soft on him or her. Do not humiliate him. Help him out if he or she feels troubled and let him or her feel more at ease.

When you feel that the opponent is completely wrong, don't encourage him to do any more wrong and guide him toward the correct path in a way so that his pride does not get hurt.

Ways of applying this method:

Restrain yourself to avoid making him or her feel embarrassed about the whole situation where he or she thinks everyone is judging them. Help them overcome it and make it feel like nothing about it is a big deal.

Principle 6: Praise the slightest improvement and praise every improvement. Be "hearty in your approbation and lavish in your praise."

When you see someone developing at least minimal improvement you need to encourage him for doing a great job. Even if it is not that big of a deal, you still need to praise him. It will help him to do more and in the future, he will be motivated to gain more than that.

You will be a good leader if you encourage people to do what they think they can't do. You need to make them believe that they are capable of doing it. Praise and encourage them in every possible way.

Ways of applying this method:

This process will be more effective if you set targets for them. Whenever they reach their targets, give them some sincere compliments or small gifts if possible.

Principle 7: Give the other person a fine reputation to live up to.

To make others work effectively, you need to make them believe that they are capable enough to do that work. You need to build a reputation for them and remind them again and again about it. The goal is that they work to fulfill the expectation to hold onto that reputation.

Ways of applying this method:

Let them know that you know their good qualities and how much you are counting on them.

Offer them sincere admiration so that they feel how valuable their contributions are.

Principle 8: Use encouragement. Make the fault seem easy to correct.

Never point out people's inability. It will just make them give up on work and make it worse. If you want the best from them, you need to make them believe that they are the best at what they do. Encourage them to work effectively and when they make mistakes, do not curse them but encourage them to correct it.

Ways of applying this method:

If it's hard to reach the goal at once for them, you need to divide the task into smaller goals so that they can take baby steps towards it. Do not use discouraging words and let them down. Guide them properly with encouragement for their efforts.

Principle 9: Make the other person happy about doing the thing you suggest.

People will listen to you when you can provide them with what they want. You need to make the effort to gain their satisfaction and happiness in order to make them do what you ask.

Ways of applying this method:

Follow the given methods for effective results:

- Never make false promises. Tell them you will provide what you can and do your best to follow through.
- Do not let your selfish desires get in the way.
- Be specific about the work you need others to do.
- Clearly state the benefits they will receive from the work.

Conclusion

How to Win Friends and Influence People is a great book which will provide you with all the necessary methods you need to know to develop your social interactions. Though this book is established for people who are in business, people from all classes can use the advice to enrich their lifestyle. This book will save you if you are having troubles with your communication skills.

***We thank you for buying the book and really hope that it will benefit you. We also want to provide you with the best summary books possible. Would you consider posting a review for us online? In addition to providing feedback, online reviews can help other customers learn who we are and about the books we offer. They are also a great way to give referrals to your family and friends.

***To find out more about other summary books, please visit the <u>Amazon Author Page</u> of [<u>Napoleon Hook</u>]. We will be adding more titles soon so please click the "<u>+Follow</u>" button to stay up-to-date.

Check Out Other Summaries

1- SUMMARY OF The Subtle Art of Not Giving a F*ck by Mark Manson— *Napoleon Hook*

This book isn't like the majority of self-help books. The key element of this book is that it avoids all the sugar-coated advice; it makes you realize that it's ok to not be optimistic at times! You will learn how to not care about everything around you.

This out of the ordinary, yet ever so helpful book is Mark's comical way of teaching you people how to confront the problems that are destined to be on your path; moreover he uses his own life examples to make us see how to live beyond our restrictions and limits.

Reference link: https://www.amazon.com/dp/171807204X

2-SUMMARY OF The 7 Habits of Highly Effective People by Stephen R. Covey: Powerful Lessons in Personal Change— *Napoleon Hook*

This book guides you through each habit step-by-step:

- *Habit 1: Be Proactive*
- *Habit 2: Begin With The End In Mind*
- *Habit 3: Put First Things First*
- *Habit 4: Think Win-Win*
- *Habit 5: Seek First To Understand Then Be Understood*
- *Habit 6: Synergize*
- *Habit 7: Sharpen The Saw*

Reference link: https://www.amazon.com/dp/1717787916

3-SUMMARY: Measure What Matters by John Doerr – *Napoleon Hook*

In *Measure What Matters* by John Doerr, he defines and makes a case for OKRs (objectives and key results) to direct a company toward success.

OKRs bring a sense of order to the goal-setting process of organizations.

The four superpowers of OKRs include (1) focus and commit, (2) align and connect, (3) track, and (4) stretch. These objectives drive companies toward a high-performance level.

The author uses the examples of Google, Intel, Bono, the Gates Foundation, and many others to signify the usefulness of OKRs. The book makes it clear how any organization can benefit from OKRs to achieve greatness by aiming effectively.

Reference link: https://www.amazon.com/dp/1718061684

4-SUMMARY OF Unlimited Memory by Kevin Horsley: How to Use Advanced Learning Strategies to Learn Faster, Remember More and be More Productive– *Napoleon Hook*

Unlimited Memory is a book that gives you control over your memory. The principles and methods discussed to give you insight into the workings of the mind, and how to utilize it for a powerful and effective memory. Memory improvement is a matter of making a decision to improve the memory. It is a conscious and deliberate effort on your part to stop making excuses for a bad memory. Excuses are for failures.

Reference link: https://www.amazon.com/dp/1717751512

THE END!

Made in the USA
San Bernardino, CA
23 August 2018